**HAL•LEONARD INSTRUMENTAL PLAY-ALONG**

**HORN**

# CONTENTS

To access audio visit:
**www.halleonard.com/mylibrary**

Enter Code
6553-4061-6387-7960

Audio Arrangements by Peter Deneff

ISBN 978-1-4950-2557-0

**HAL•LEONARD® CORPORATION**

7777 W. BLUEMOUND RD. P.O. BOX 13819 MILWAUKEE, WI 53213

For all works contained herein:
Unauthorized copying, arranging, adapting, recording, Internet posting, public performance,
or other distribution of the printed or recorded music in this publication is an infringement of copyright.
Infringers are liable under the law.

Visit Hal Leonard Online at
**www.halleonard.com**

# ALL I WANT FOR CHRISTMAS IS YOU

Horn

Words and Music by MARIAH CAREY
and WALTER AFANASIEFF

Copyright © 1994 RYE SONGS, SONY/ATV MUSIC PUBLISHING LLC, TAMAL VISTA MUSIC and WALLYWORLD MUSIC
All Rights for RYE SONGS Controlled and Administered by SONGS OF UNIVERSAL, INC.
All Rights for SONY/ATV MUSIC PUBLISHING LLC, TAMAL VISTA MUSIC and WALLYWORLD MUSIC Administered by
SONY/ATV MUSIC PUBLISHING LLC, 424 Church Street, Suite 1200, Nashville, TN 37219
All Rights Reserved   Used by Permission

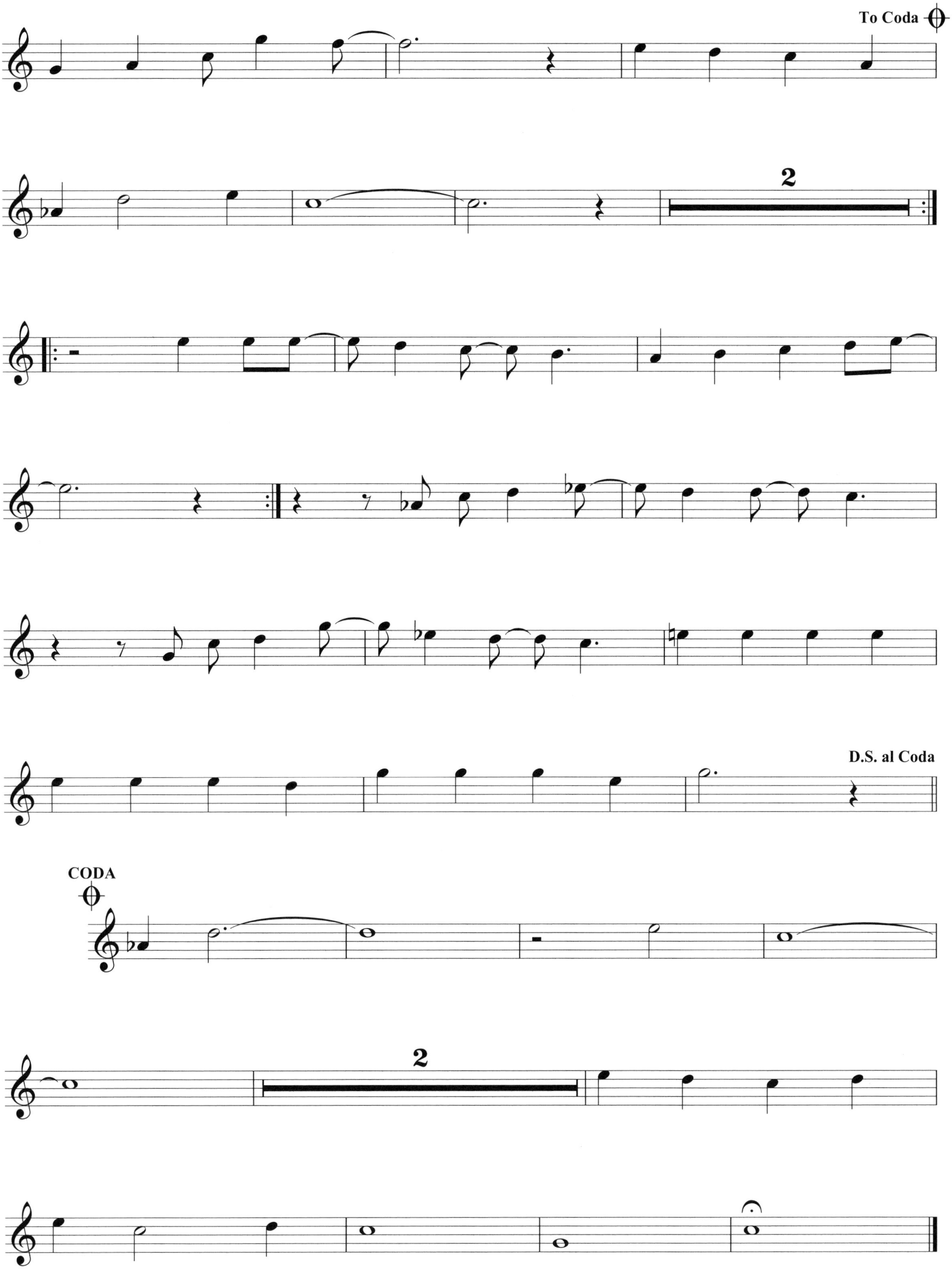
To Coda
2
D.S. al Coda
CODA
2

# THE CHRISTMAS WALTZ

HORN

Words by SAMMY CAHN
Music by JULE STYNE

© 1954 (Renewed) PRODUCERS MUSIC PUBLISHING CO., INC. and CAHN MUSIC CO.
All Rights for PRODUCERS MUSIC PUBLISHING CO., INC. Administered by CHAPPELL & CO., INC.
All Rights for CAHN MUSIC CO. Administered by IMAGEM SOUNDS
All Rights Reserved   Used by Permisison

# HAPPY HOLIDAY
from the Motion Picture Irving Berlin's HOLIDAY INN

Horn

Words and Music by
IRVING BERLIN

© Copyright 1941, 1942 by Irving Berlin
Copyright Renewed
International Copyright Secured   All Rights Reserved

# I WONDER AS I WANDER

HORN

By JOHN JACOB NILES

Copyright © 1934 (Renewed) by G. Schirmer, Inc. (ASCAP), New York, NY
International Copyright Secured   All Rights Reserved
Reprinted by Permission

# I'LL BE HOME FOR CHRISTMAS

Horn

Words and Music by KIM GANNON
and WALTER KENT

**Slowly, with feeling**

© Copyright 1943 by Gannon & Kent Music Co., Inc., Beverly Hills, CA
Copyright Renewed
International Copyright Secured   All Rights Reserved

# LET IT SNOW! LET IT SNOW! LET IT SNOW!

HORN

Words by SAMMY CAHN
Music by JULE STYNE

© 1945 (Renewed) PRODUCERS MUSIC PUBLISHING CO., INC. and CAHN MUSIC CO.
All Rights for PRODUCERS MUSIC PUBLISHING CO., INC. Administered by CHAPPELL & CO., INC.
All Rights for CAHN MUSIC CO. Administered by IMAGEM SOUNDS
All Rights Reserved   Used by Permisison

# MARY, DID YOU KNOW?

Horn

Words and Music by MARK LOWRY
and BUDDY GREENE

© 1991 Word Music, LLC and Rufus Music (administered at CapitolCMGPublishing.com)
All Rights Reserved   Used by Permission

# THE MOST WONDERFUL TIME OF THE YEAR

HORN

Words and Music by EDDIE POLA
and GEORGE WYLE

Copyright © 1963 Barnaby Music Corp.
Copyright Renewed
Administered by Lichelle Music Company
International Copyright Secured   All Rights Reserved

# MY FAVORITE THINGS
from THE SOUND OF MUSIC

Horn

Lyrics by OSCAR HAMMERSTEIN II
Music by RICHARD RODGERS

Copyright © 1959 by Richard Rodgers and Oscar Hammerstein II
Copyright Renewed
Williamson Music, a Division of Rodgers & Hammerstein: an Imagem Company, owner of publication and allied rights throughout the world
International Copyright Secured   All Rights Reserved

# SILVER BELLS
from the Paramount Picture THE LEMON DROP KID

HORN

Words and Music by JAY LIVINGSTON
and RAY EVANS

Copyright © 1950 Sony/ATV Music Publishing LLC
Copyright Renewed
All Rights Administered by Sony/ATV Music Publishing LLC, 424 Church Street, Suite 1200, Nashville, TN 37219
International Copyright Secured   All Rights Reserved

# THIS CHRISTMAS

Horn

Words and Music by DONNY HATHAWAY
and NADINE McKINNOR

Copyright © 1970 by Universal Music - MGB Songs, Kuumba Music Publishing and Crystal Raisin Music
Copyright Renewed
All Rights for Kuumba Music Publishing Administered by Universal Music - MGB Songs
International Copyright Secured   All Rights Reserved

# WHITE CHRISTMAS

from the Motion Picture Irving Berlin's HOLIDAY INN

HORN

Words and Music by
IRVING BERLIN

© Copyright 1940, 1942 by Irving Berlin
Copyright Renewed
International Copyright Secured   All Rights Reserved

# HAL•LEONARD INSTRUMENTAL PLAY-ALONG

Your favorite songs are arranged just for solo instrumentalists with this outstanding series. Each book includes a great full-accompaniment play-along CD so you can sound just like a pro! Check out www.halleonard.com to see all the titles available.

## Disney Greats

Arabian Nights • Hawaiian Roller Coaster Ride • It's a Small World • Look Through My Eyes • Yo Ho (A Pirate's Life for Me) • and more.

| | | | |
|---|---|---|---|
| ___ | 00841934 | Flute | $12.95 |
| ___ | 00841935 | Clarinet | $12.95 |
| ___ | 00841936 | Alto Sax | $12.95 |
| ___ | 00841937 | Tenor Sax | $12.95 |
| ___ | 00841938 | Trumpet | $12.95 |
| ___ | 00841939 | Horn | $12.95 |
| ___ | 00841940 | Trombone | $12.95 |
| ___ | 00841941 | Violin | $12.95 |
| ___ | 00841942 | Viola | $12.95 |
| ___ | 00841943 | Cello | $12.95 |
| ___ | 00842078 | Oboe | $12.95 |

## Great Themes

Bella's Lullaby • Chariots of Fire • Get Smart • Hawaii Five-O Theme • I Love Lucy • The Odd Couple • Spanish Flea • and more.

| | | | |
|---|---|---|---|
| ___ | 00842468 | Flute | $12.99 |
| ___ | 00842469 | Clarinet | $12.99 |
| ___ | 00842470 | Alto Sax | $12.99 |
| ___ | 00842471 | Tenor Sax | $12.99 |
| ___ | 00842472 | Trumpet | $12.99 |
| ___ | 00842473 | Horn | $12.99 |
| ___ | 00842474 | Trombone | $12.99 |
| ___ | 00842475 | Violin | $12.99 |
| ___ | 00842476 | Viola | $12.99 |
| ___ | 00842477 | Cello | $12.99 |

## Coldplay

Clocks • Every Teardrop Is a Waterfall • Fix You • In My Place • Lost! • Paradise • The Scientist • Speed of Sound • Trouble • Violet Hill • Viva La Vida • Yellow.

| | | | |
|---|---|---|---|
| ___ | 00103337 | Flute | $12.99 |
| ___ | 00103338 | Clarinet | $12.99 |
| ___ | 00103339 | Alto Sax | $12.99 |
| ___ | 00103340 | Tenor Sax | $12.99 |
| ___ | 00103341 | Trumpet | $12.99 |
| ___ | 00103342 | Horn | $12.99 |
| ___ | 00103343 | Trombone | $12.99 |
| ___ | 00103344 | Violin | $12.99 |
| ___ | 00103345 | Viola | $12.99 |
| ___ | 00103346 | Cello | $12.99 |

## Popular Hits

Breakeven • Fireflies • Halo • Hey, Soul Sister • I Gotta Feeling • I'm Yours • Need You Now • Poker Face • Viva La Vida • You Belong with Me • and more.

| | | | |
|---|---|---|---|
| ___ | 00842511 | Flute | $12.99 |
| ___ | 00842512 | Clarinet | $12.99 |
| ___ | 00842513 | Alto Sax | $12.99 |
| ___ | 00842514 | Tenor Sax | $12.99 |
| ___ | 00842515 | Trumpet | $12.99 |
| ___ | 00842516 | Horn | $12.99 |
| ___ | 00842517 | Trombone | $12.99 |
| ___ | 00842518 | Violin | $12.99 |
| ___ | 00842519 | Viola | $12.99 |
| ___ | 00842520 | Cello | $12.99 |

## Lennon & McCartney Favorites

All You Need Is Love • A Hard Day's Night • Here, There and Everywhere • Hey Jude • Let It Be • Nowhere Man • Penny Lane • She Loves You • When I'm Sixty-Four • and more.

| | | | |
|---|---|---|---|
| ___ | 00842600 | Flute | $12.99 |
| ___ | 00842601 | Clarinet | $12.99 |
| ___ | 00842602 | Alto Sax | $12.99 |
| ___ | 00842603 | Tenor Sax | $12.99 |
| ___ | 00842604 | Trumpet | $12.99 |
| ___ | 00842605 | Horn | $12.99 |
| ___ | 00842606 | Trombone | $12.99 |
| ___ | 00842607 | Violin | $12.99 |
| ___ | 00842608 | Viola | $12.99 |
| ___ | 00842609 | Cello | $12.99 |

## Women of Pop

Bad Romance • Jar of Hearts • Mean • My Life Would Suck Without You • Our Song • Rolling in the Deep • Single Ladies (Put a Ring on It) • Teenage Dream • and more.

| | | | |
|---|---|---|---|
| ___ | 00842650 | Flute | $12.99 |
| ___ | 00842651 | Clarinet | $12.99 |
| ___ | 00842652 | Alto Sax | $12.99 |
| ___ | 00842653 | Tenor Sax | $12.99 |
| ___ | 00842654 | Trumpet | $12.99 |
| ___ | 00842655 | Horn | $12.99 |
| ___ | 00842656 | Trombone | $12.99 |
| ___ | 00842657 | Violin | $12.99 |
| ___ | 00842658 | Viola | $12.99 |
| ___ | 00842659 | Cello | $12.99 |

## Movie Music

And All That Jazz • Come What May • I Am a Man of Constant Sorrow • I Believe I Can Fly • I Walk the Line • Seasons of Love • Theme from *Spider Man* • and more.

| | | | |
|---|---|---|---|
| ___ | 00842090 | Clarinet | $10.95 |
| ___ | 00842091 | Alto Sax | $10.95 |
| ___ | 00842092 | Tenor Sax | $10.95 |
| ___ | 00842094 | Horn | $10.95 |
| ___ | 00842095 | Trombone | $10.95 |
| ___ | 00842096 | Violin | $10.95 |
| ___ | 00842097 | Viola | $10.95 |

## TV Favorites

The Addams Family Theme • The Brady Bunch • Green Acres Theme • Happy Days • Johnny's Theme • Linus and Lucy • Theme from the Simpsons • and more.

| | | | |
|---|---|---|---|
| ___ | 00842079 | Flute | $10.95 |
| ___ | 00842080 | Clarinet | $10.95 |
| ___ | 00842081 | Alto Sax | $10.95 |
| ___ | 00842082 | Tenor Sax | $10.95 |
| ___ | 00842083 | Trumpet | $10.95 |
| ___ | 00842084 | Horn | $10.95 |
| ___ | 00842085 | Trombone | $10.95 |
| ___ | 00842087 | Viola | $10.95 |

## Wicked

As Long As You're Mine • Dancing Through Life • Defying Gravity • For Good • I'm Not That Girl • Popular • The Wizard and I • and more.

| | | | |
|---|---|---|---|
| ___ | 00842236 | Flute | $11.95 |
| ___ | 00842237 | Clarinet | $11.95 |
| ___ | 00842238 | Alto Saxophone | $11.95 |
| ___ | 00842239 | Tenor Saxophone | $11.95 |
| ___ | 00842240 | Trumpet | $11.95 |
| ___ | 00842241 | Horn | $11.95 |
| ___ | 00842242 | Trombone | $11.95 |
| ___ | 00842243 | Violin | $11.95 |
| ___ | 00842244 | Viola | $11.95 |
| ___ | 00842245 | Cello | $11.95 |

FOR MORE INFORMATION, SEE YOUR LOCAL MUSIC DEALER, OR WRITE TO:

HAL•LEONARD® CORPORATION
7777 W. BLUEMOUND RD. P.O. BOX 13819 MILWAUKEE, WI 53213

Prices, contents, and availability subject to change without notice.
Disney characters and artwork © Disney Enterprises, Inc.